Stop!
the Watch

★ A BOOK OF ★
EVERYDAY, ORDINARY,
ANYBODY OLYMPICS

★★★★★

by the editors
of Klutz Press

Klutz Press

Acknowledgments

Mark Palmer
Jodi Kantor
All the Klutzes, especially Kathy Harrington
and Tom Borthwick.

Illustrations:

Ed Taber

Design and Production:

Carrington Design

Book printed in the United States.
Stopwatch manufactured in Taiwan.

✎ Write Us

Klutz Press is an independent publisher located in Palo Alto,
California and staffed entirely by real humans. We would love
to hear your comments regarding this or any of our books.

If you are having trouble locating additional copies of this or
any other Klutz books, give us a call at (415) 857-0888 for the
name of your nearest Klutz retailer. Should they be out of stock,
additional books can be ordered from our mail order catalogue.
See back page.

Klutz Press
2121 Staunton Court
Palo Alto, CA 94306

ISBN 1-878257-52-8

Table of Contents

Are You A World Champion?

All of the Official World Records printed in this book were set by the extraordinary people at Klutz Press headquarters in Palo Alto, California. They are official because we say so, and they are accurate because we timed them ourselves.

However.

If you can beat one of them, send in your time, preferably with a note from your mother or someone like that. If we believe it, and if we can't beat it ourselves, we'll include it in the next printing.

Our address: Klutz Press
World Records Dept.
2121 Staunton Court
Palo Alto, CA 94306

Introduction

Grip your new stopwatch tightly and stare at it for a few moments. Treasure it. Your life, which used to be little more than a dull series of household activities and chores, is about to be completely transformed.

Let me explain with a pair of examples.

Let's say you're in the habit of going out in the morning to fetch the paper. Typically, this is not the highlight of your day. But that was before. Now, you have the means to turn a formerly mindless chore like fetching the paper into an incredible Domestic Olympic Event. Do it for time! Every morning! Set records and put them up on the fridge!

O r perhaps you're a parent. Perhaps you encounter a certain degree of resistance when bedtime rolls around. Perhaps this has been a source of some friction in your house.

Well, you'll be glad to hear your problems in this sensitive area are over. Now you can completely repackage the whole ugly mess. How? Turn bedtime into a fabulous bedroom decathlon..."*Toothbrush for Time*" (slowest wins) ...."*PJ Quick Change*"...."*Close Eyes and Fall Asleep World Records.*" The possibilities are staggering. Post the best times on the wall by the door and every evening,

"Go for the gold!"

Don't Read This Section!!!

This is the section on how to work your stopwatch, but it's quite boring to read so stop right here unless you're really having problems. Just punch the buttons aimlessly and look at what the numbers do. It's pretty self-evident. A picture follows:

The *right button* starts and stops the watch. The *left button* sets the watch back to zero, so long as you push it when the numbers are stopped and the word "stop" appears by them.

Push to go back to zero.

Push to Start, then push to Stop.

This is all you need to know. Push the right button when you start your event, and push it again when you're done. Read the time and then push the left button to set yourself back to zero. That's it. Almost too simple for words.

But maybe you should
keep reading anyway.

Nothing is so simple you can't mess it up. When you use the left button to stop the watch (instead of the right one like you're supposed to) the display will stop (and the word "lap" will appear), but the insides of the watch will keep right on running. Then, when you push the left button again, the *display* will jump forward to whatever it would have been if you hadn't ever pushed the left button in the first place.

People normally stop the watch with the left button (it's called the "lap function") only when they get fuddled and forget the right way to do it. However, some advanced stop-watch users like to "peek" at the watch when they're midway into an event. The lap function gives them a way to do this.

Replacing the battery: The battery should last a year. When yours finally expires, you'll need to replace it with a micro-cell SG3. Unscrew the back, slip out the dead battery and slip in the new. Replace the back, and it should be good for another year. Watch batteries are generally available at jewelers, but you can always order more from us (address in the back of the book).

WRONG

RIGHT

Solo Domestic Events
You against the

These are the events that you'll need to start your solo career in Domestic Olympics. As you test yourself in each, *you have to record your time in pencil.* This is crucial. Otherwise you won't be able to set personal records, nor will any competition be possible. (Your best time for tying both shoes is 18 seconds? Fine, but how does that stack up against anyone else's best time?)

Use the blanks on each page and fill them in. You'll notice that frequently we have printed our own "in-house" records. We have set these records here ourselves, under tightly controlled conditions, right at corporate Klutz headquarters. Don't be concerned if you can't compete with these records. Because of the extraordinary kind of people we are, we suspect these numbers represent the extreme limits to human achievement. Ordinary mortals would be doing well to even come close. So don't be disappointed.

NO PRACTICE ALLOWED A number of these events have to be timed with no benefit of any practice. If you are the sort of person you can trust, just read the instructions and immediately punch the clock and start. If you are not the sort of person you can trust, skip all the mental events until you can get someone else to read them and he or she can be your timer.

This is your competition

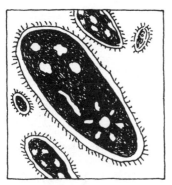

Before working at Klutz

After Klutz

Speed Punching

The purest event. Start and stop the watch as quickly as you can, *one hand only.*

A variant: Start the watch, but pass it around your body before you stop it.

(variant)

_____ / _____

My very first effort.

_____ / _____

My best time _after_ practice.

_____ / _____

My _____'s feeble effort.
(friend, sister, brother, etc.)

WORLD RECORD

Set at sea level
at Klutz H.Q.

0.02 sec.

Can you beat it?
Can you even come close?

Adrenaline Addition

C ount to 126 by 7s, out loud and with *no* practice.

MENTAL EVENT

_____/_____

My time.

_____/_____

My _____'s feeble effort.
(friend, sister, brother, etc.)

WORLD RECORD

Set at sea level
at Klutz H.Q.

9.66 sec.

Can you beat it?
Can you even come close?

Writing for Time

Write the following verse:

By the shores of Gitche Gumee,
By the shining Big-Sea-Water,
Stood the wigwam of Nokomis,
Daughter of the Moon, Nokomis.

If somebody else can't read it on the first try, with no hints, it doesn't count.

_____

My very first effort.

_____

My best time <u>after</u> practice.

_____

My _____'s feeble effort.
(friend, sister, brother, etc.)

WORLD RECORD

Set at sea level
at Klutz H.Q.

32.5 sec.

Can you beat it?
Can you even come close?

Calisthenics by the Clock

Touch your toes five times, do six jumping jacks, turn around four times, then stop and say the "Pledge of Allegiance."

_____
My very first effort.

_____
My best time <u>after</u> practice.

_____
My _____'s feeble effort.
   (friend, sister, brother, etc.)

WORLD RECORD

Set at sea level
at Klutz H.Q.

15.14_{sec.}

Can you beat it?
Can you even come close?

WARNING!
No practice allowed.
Start the clock
NOW!

Teeth Counting

Count your teeth twice, and get the same number both times.

Start the clock NOW!

_____

My time.

_____

My _____'s feeble effort.
(friend, sister, brother, etc.)

WORLD RECORD

Set at sea level
at Klutz H.Q.

20.95 sec.

Can you beat it?
Can you even come close?

Shoelace Tying

Start with your shoes on and laced, but untied.

_____

My very first effort.

_____

My best time after practice.

_____

My _____'s feeble effort.
(friend, sister, brother, etc.)

Singing

Sing "Happy
Birthday" to
Rumpelstiltskin five
times.

Has to be out loud, completely understandable
and bear some resemblance to music.

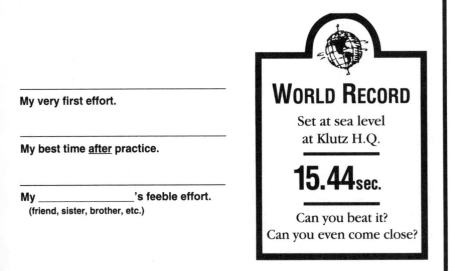

_____
My very first effort.

_____
My best time <u>after</u> practice.

_____
My _____'s feeble effort.
(friend, sister, brother, etc.)

WORLD RECORD
Set at sea level
at Klutz H.Q.

15.44 sec.

Can you beat it?
Can you even come close?

Memory for Speed

WARNING!
No practice allowed.
Start the clock **NOW!**

MENTAL EVENT

Name five African countries and your second-grade teacher. No thinking beforehand!

Remember, you only get one try at this one!

_____

My time.

_____

My _____'s feeble effort.
(friend, sister, brother, etc.)

WORLD RECORD

Set at sea level
at Klutz H.Q.

5.53 sec.

Can you beat it?
Can you even come close?

Posture for Speed

Walk up the stairs with a book balanced on your head.

One flight of stairs, preferably with a landing. If the book falls, start over.

My very first effort.

My best time after practice.

My _____'s feeble effort.
(friend, sister, brother, etc.)

WORLD RECORD
Set at sea level
at Klutz H.Q.

2.37 sec.

Can you beat it?
Can you even come close?

Dash Art

Draw a recognizable gorilla. You have to be able to show it to someone else, and with no prompting from you at all, he or she has to say "Nice gorilla."

The Winner

WORLD RECORD

Set at sea level
at Klutz H.Q.

50.27 sec.

Can you beat it?
Can you even come close?

_____
My very first effort.

_____
My best time _after_ practice.

_____
My _____'s feeble effort.
(friend, sister, brother, etc.)

Fire Drill

Go in one door of a car, out another, and then run all the way around the car.

START

My very first effort.

My best time **after** practice.

My _____'s feeble effort.
(friend, sister, brother, etc.)

WORLD RECORD
Set at sea level
at Klutz H.Q.

7.85sec.

Can you beat it?
Can you even come close?

Floss Writing

rite the word "banana" with dental floss.
You have to be able to show your creation to someone else, and he or she has to be able to read it on the first try. No hints.

_____
My very first effort.

_____
My best time <u>after</u> practice.

_____
My _____'s feeble effort.
   (friend, sister, brother, etc.)

WORLD RECORD

Set at sea level
at Klutz H.Q.

_____

24.88sec.

_____

Can you beat it?
Can you even come close?

Speed Reading

Find a magazine.
Sit down with it.
Start the clock.
Open the maga-
zine and find the word "run."

_____

My time.

_____

My _____'s feeble effort.
(friend, sister, brother, etc.)

WORLD RECORD

Set at sea level
at Klutz H.Q.

19.53 sec.

Can you beat it?
Can you even come close?

Say the Magic Word

Get an unsuspecting person to say the word "special" in a conversation with you. You can't use it yourself, or say anything about what you're trying to do.

_____
My time.

_____
My _____'s feeble effort.
(friend, sister, brother, etc.)

WORLD RECORD

Set at sea level
at Klutz H.Q.

24.13 sec.

Can you beat it?
Can you even come close?

Channel Surfing

Turn on the TV and flip through the channels until you see a cat, or someone doing something illegal.

My time.
_____

My _____'s feeble effort.
(friend, sister, brother, etc.)

WORLD RECORD

Set at sea level
at Klutz H.Q.

20.15sec.

Can you beat it?
Can you even come close?

Raisin Tossing

Toss five raisins in a row into the air and catch them all in your mouth. No misses.

WORLD RECORD

Set at sea level
at Klutz H.Q.

8.97 sec.

Can you beat it?
Can you even come close?

_____
My very first effort.

_____
My best time after practice.

_____
My _____'s feeble effort.
  (friend, sister, brother, etc.)

Barely Cracking the Book

Open a book to page 73. Start with the book closed in your hands.

_____

My very first effort.

_____

My best time _after_ practice.

_____

My _____'s feeble effort.
  (friend, sister, brother, etc.)

WORLD RECORD

Set at sea level
at Klutz H.Q.

1.11 sec.

Can you beat it?
Can you even come close?

Name That Tune!

Start the clock.
Whistle
"O Susannah."

Stop the clock when someone can name it. No Hints.

_____
My very first effort.

_____
My best time <u>after</u> practice.

_____
My _____**'s feeble effort.**
(friend, sister, brother, etc.)

WORLD RECORD
Set at sea level
at Klutz H.Q.

8.63 sec.

Can you beat it?
Can you even come close?

Finger Snapping

*S*nap your fingers 24 times. One hand.

_____

My very first effort.

_____

My best time _after_ practice.

_____

My _____'s feeble effort.
  (friend, sister, brother, etc.)

WORLD RECORD

Set at sea level
at Klutz H.Q.

5.35sec.

Can you beat it?
Can you even come close?

Under Bed Crawling

Crawl under-
neath a bed.

Start by standing beside it. Crawl all the way under-
neath it. Stop the clock when you are standing up on
the other side.

_____
My very first effort.

_____
My best time _after_ practice.

_____
My _____'s feeble effort.
   (friend, sister, brother, etc.)

WORLD RECORD

Set at sea level
at Klutz H.Q.

4.53 sec.

Can you beat it?
Can you even come close?

Star Spangled Counting

N ame the 15th word in the *"Star Spangled Banner."* Hint: The first word is *"O."*

_____

My time.

_____

My _____'s feeble effort.
(friend, sister, brother, etc.)

WORLD RECORD

Set at sea level
at Klutz H.Q.

6.66SEC.

Can you beat it?
Can you even come close?

Shoelace Switching

Switch shoelaces and re-tie them both. Start with both on and tied.

My very first effort.

My best time _after_ practice.

My _____'s feeble effort.
(friend, sister, brother, etc.)

Affection for Time

Get your mother to say "Stop bothering me." No fair telling her anything about what you're trying to do.

My time.

My _____'s feeble effort.
(friend, sister, brother, etc.)

WORLD RECORD
Set at sea level
at Klutz H.Q.

7.59sec.

Can you beat it?
Can you even come close?

ABCs for Speed

Recite the alphabet out loud and understandably.

_____

My very first effort.

_____

My best time _after_ practice.

_____

My _____**'s feeble effort.**
(friend, sister, brother, etc.)

WORLD RECORD

Set at sea level
at Klutz H.Q.

2.77 sec.

Can you beat it?
Can you even come close?

Get Very Lucky for Time

Flip a coin until you get either heads or tails five times straight.

_____

My very first effort.

_____

My best time.

_____

My _____'s feeble effort.
(friend, sister, brother, etc.)

WORLD RECORD

Set at sea level
at Klutz H.Q.

_____

20.03sec.

_____

Can you beat it?
Can you even come close?

One Foot Marathon

Stand on one foot with both eyes closed. You may not touch anything for support, or hop around.

My very first effort.

My best time.

My _____'s **feeble effort.**
(friend, sister, brother, etc.)

Meet the Clock
Solo Events

These events are a little different. Here the idea is to do something in a pre-set period of time. Exactly. *But you can't look at your watch while you're doing it.*

For example: Say the event is "Hold your breath for 23 seconds exactly." If you go over or under 23, the penalty is the same—one point per second. Write your penalty points in the space provided and you can compete with friends.

Tickling for Time

Tickle the roof of your mouth with your finger for 10 seconds. Exactly.

Remember: No fair looking at your watch.

penalty points

_____

My very first effort.　　penalty points

_____

My best time.　　penalty points

_____

My _____'s feeble effort.
(friend, sister, brother, etc.)

Precision Hollering

Holler the word "Eeeeeeeeeeeeeellllllllllllllllskin" continuously, without taking a breath, for 17 seconds. Exactly.

_____ **penalty points**

My very first effort.

_____ **penalty points**

My best time.

_____ **penalty points**

My _____'s feeble effort.
   (friend, sister, brother, etc.)

37

Reading by the Clock

Start the clock. Read an entire page from a grown-up book out loud. Stop the clock.

_____

My very first effort.

_____

My best time.

_____

My _____'s feeble effort.
  (friend, sister, brother, etc.)

WORLD RECORD

Set at sea level
at Klutz H.Q.

1:50.81

Can you beat it?
Can you even come close?

Back Pain for Time

Touch the palms of your hands to the floor for 11 seconds. You have to be standing up, and bend the knees as much as you have to.

_____ **penalty points**

My very first effort.

_____ **penalty points**

My best time.

_____ **penalty points**

My _____'s feeble effort.
  (friend, sister, brother, etc.)

Speed Sitting

Sit in a chair, don't move, don't say a thing, don't even think for exactly 60 seconds.

Tic-Tic-Tic

_____ penalty points

My very first effort.

_____ penalty points

My best time.

_____ penalty points

My _____'s feeble effort.
   (friend, sister, brother, etc.)

Living for Time

Start your clock and go on about your day, doing whatever it is you normally do. Don't give a thought to the fact that you are now living for time.

When exactly five minutes are up, holler "NOW" at the top of your lungs. Check the watch to see how you did. Remember: One penalty point per second. Doesn't matter if you went over or under.

<u>   </u> `penalty points`

My very first effort.

<u>   </u> `penalty points`

My best time.

<u>   </u> `penalty points`

My _____'s feeble effort.
(friend, sister, brother, etc.)

Counting on the Clock

Count by 6s until 12 seconds have elapsed. Exactly.

_____ | penalty points |

My very first effort.

_____ | penalty points |

My best time.

_____ | penalty points |

My _____'s feeble effort.
    (friend, sister, brother, etc.)

42

The One-Minute Minstrel

Sing *"99 Bottles of Beer on the Wall"* until two things happen. One: 60 seconds have passed (exactly). And two: You reach 90 bottles. Both things have to happen at exactly the same time.

_____ penalty points

My very first effort.

_____ penalty points

My best time.

_____ penalty points

My _____'s feeble effort.
(friend, sister, brother, etc.)

Fly, Math and Destroy

1. Start clock.
2. Fold a paper airplane and successfully launch.
3. Pick it up. Flatten it out and do a multiplication problem. Both numbers have to be over one thousand.
4. Tear sheet into 11 pieces exactly.
5. Stop clock.

_____

My very first effort.

_____

My best time.

_____

My _____**'s feeble effort.**
(friend, sister, brother, etc.)

WORLD RECORD

Set at sea level
at Klutz H.Q.

35.38 sec.

Can you beat it?
Can you even come close?

Flip, Switch and Phone

1. Start the clock.

2. Flip a coin until you get four somethings in a row.

3. Switch your socks (start with shoes on and finish with them on, but you don't have to re-tie the laces.)

4. Crawl over to the phone. Call the Time Lady. Stop the clock when she says "Exactly."

_____

My very first effort.

_____

My best time.

_____

My _____'s feeble effort.
(friend, sister, brother, etc.)

WORLD RECORD

Set at sea level
at Klutz H.Q.

1:30.7

Can you beat it?
Can you even come close?

Two-Person Team Events

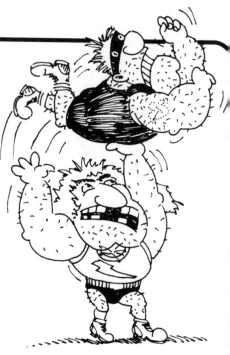

These are events designed for one stopwatch and two people. Partners cooperate to set records. Competition, for you red-blooded competitors, would have to be between teams.

Leap Frogging

Leapfrog over one another seven times.

_____
Our very first effort.

_____
Our best time.

_____
Another team's feeble effort.

Start, Pass and Stop

Start the watch and hand it to your partner, who has to stop it.

_____

Our very first effort.

_____

Our best time.

_____

Another team's feeble effort.

WORLD RECORD

Set at sea level
at Klutz H.Q.

0.44sec.

Can you beat it?
Can you even come close?

Partner Lugging

Pick up your partner (or vice versa, whichever is more realistic) and carry him or her ten steps.

_____
Our very first effort.

_____
Our best time.

_____
Another team's feeble effort.

WORLD RECORD

Set at sea level
at Klutz H.Q.

4.22 sec.

Can you beat it?
Can you even come close?

Jingle Bells

Sing the first verse of "Jingle Bells" alternating each word between partners.

_____

Our very first effort.

_____

Our best time.

_____

Another team's feeble effort.

WORLD RECORD

Set at sea level
at Klutz H.Q.

7.4 sec.

Can you beat it?
Can you even come close?

Hot Potato

Without using your hands or mouths, pass the watch back and forth four times, between you and your partner. You may use the loop, but no furniture or any tools. If the watch touches the ground, start over.

_____
Our very first effort.

_____
Our best time.

_____
Another team's feeble effort.

WORLD RECORD

Set at sea level
at Klutz H.Q.

3.16 sec.

Can you beat it?
Can you even come close?

Name that Breakfast

tart the clock. On a piece of paper, record everything you had for breakfast this morning. Hand it to your partner who has to be able to read it out loud. Stop the clock when he or she finishes. No hints.

_____

Our very first effort.

_____

Our best time.

_____

Another team's feeble effort.

WORLD RECORD

Set at sea level
at Klutz H.Q.

2.94 sec.

Can you beat it?
Can you even come close?

Spelling
for Time

Name a letter. Your partner names another. Back and forth you go. The object is to spell a five-letter word. If you spell any word shorter than five letters (or longer), it doesn't count. Naturally, no hints between partners.

_____

Our very first effort.

_____

Our best time.

_____

Another team's feeble effort.

WORLD RECORD

Set at sea level
at Klutz H.Q.

4.31 sec.

Can you beat it?
Can you even come close?

Back Jacket Attack

Both of you put your jackets on backwards and zip them up. You can help each other as much as you like.

Our very first effort.

Our best time.

Another team's feeble effort.

WORLD RECORD

Set at sea level
at Klutz H.Q.

13.63 sec.

Can you beat it?
Can you even come close?

Oddball Catching

Throw something weird back and forth ten times with no drops. You have to be at least 5 feet apart.

Our very first effort.

Our best time.

Another team's feeble effort.

WORLD RECORD

Set at sea level
at Klutz H.Q.

4.63 sec.

Can you beat it?
Can you even come close?

Back and Forth Book Batting

Use hardbound books as rackets, and bat a tennis ball back and forth ten times with no drops. You have to be at least 5 feet apart.

_____

Our very first effort.

_____

Our best time.

_____

Another team's feeble effort.

WORLD RECORD

Set at sea level
at Klutz H.Q.

_____

6.88 sec.

Can you beat it?
Can you even come close?

Back Writing

Write a five-letter word on your partner's back using just your fingertip. Stop the clock when your partner guesses the word correctly. Neither of you can say anything, or give any body language hints.

Our very first effort.

Our best time.

Another team's feeble effort.

WORLD RECORD

Set at sea level at Klutz H.Q.

6.62 sec.

Can you beat it?
Can you even come close?

Shoe Relays

Take off a shoe. Start the watch. Put the shoe on your head and run around your partner five times. Give it to your partner and he or she has to do the same. Stop the clock.

_____

Our very first effort.

_____

Our best time.

_____

Another team's feeble effort.

WORLD RECORD

Set at sea level
at Klutz H.Q.

33.38 sec.

Can you beat it?
Can you even come close?

Seat Switching

Start by sitting in two chairs, at least 10 feet apart. Start the clock, crawl to the other chair and sit down while your partner does the same. Stop the clock.

_____

Our very first effort.

_____

Our best time.

_____

Another team's feeble effort.

WORLD RECORD

Set at sea level
at Klutz H.Q.

2.91 sec.

Can you beat it?
Can you even come close?

P.D.Q. Poetry

Ask six different body questions that rhyme in the following format: "How's your back, Jack?" or even better, "How's your head, Fred?"

_____

Our very first effort.

_____

Our best time.

_____

Another team's feeble effort.

WORLD RECORD

Set at sea level
at Klutz H.Q.

60.31 sec.

Can you beat it?
Can you even come close?

Back-to-Back Pass Around

Standing back-to-back, you and your partner have to pass an object that weighs as much as a bowling ball around your bodies, or over your head, five times. Can't move your feet.

_____
Our very first effort.

_____
Our best time.

_____
Another team's feeble effort.

WORLD RECORD

Set at sea level
at Klutz H.Q.

8.71 sec.

Can you beat it?
Can you even come close?

Elbow to Ear

Touch your partner's ear with your elbow. Now run around and touch his or her other ear with your other elbow. Then your partner does the same thing to you. Stop the clock.

_____
Our very first effort.

_____
Our best time.

_____
Another teams feeble effort.

WORLD RECORD

Set at sea level
at Klutz H.Q.

4.48 sec.

Can you beat it?
Can you even come close?

Double Stepping

Step on your partner's feet (one on top of the other) and hang on to him or her. Now the two of you have to walk 35 steps, and you are not allowed to touch the ground.

_____

Our very first effort.

_____

Our best time.

_____

Another team's feeble effort.

WORLD RECORD

Set at sea level
at Klutz H.Q.

13.81 sec.

Can you beat it?
Can you even come close?

Spoon Pass

Fill a spoon with water and then start the clock. Pass the spoon—no spills—back and forth ten times.

Our very first effort.

Our best time.

Another team's feeble effort.

All-Day Events

Have you ever wondered EXACTLY how much time your brother spends ragging on you in one 24-hour period? Or EXACTLY how much time you spend eating? Or how much time you spend in a complete mental haze?

Well, you now have the tools to find out this depressing information. Tomorrow morning, make sure your watch is set to zero and hang it around your neck. Pick one of the following activities and record its total time for the entire day. Just use the start/stop button over and over again, no re-setting. In the evening, look at the number and weep.

Then, gather yourself together and do a "Rest-of-My-Life" estimate. Multiply your elapsed time by the number of days left in your life (You don't know the number of days left in your life? It's easy to figure out. Here's the formula: [77 – your age] x 365 = number of

days you've got left. Of course, this is figured on average. Actual results may vary.)

Here's a grim example: You decide to total up all your bathroom time for the day and get 24 minutes and 19 seconds (or 1,459 seconds). You're 17 years old, which means you've got roughly 60 years (2,900 days) left. You multiply 1,459 seconds by 21,900 and get 31,952,100 seconds. That's how many seconds you'll be spending in a bathroom for the rest of your life.

P.S. Since there are 86,400 seconds in a day, that translates to 370 24-hour days. Think about that.

What follows is a starter list of some general activities you might want to time over the course of Your Average Day. *Note that this is a general list.* Customize it by adding activities unique to your own dynamic lifestyle.

✔ Eating

✔ Commuting

✔ Sleeping

✔ Bathroom

✔ Doing things you

definitely don't want to do

✔ Experiencing mild

emotional upset

✔ Experiencing extreme

emotional upset

- Watching TV
- Telephone
- Feeding pet
- Cleaning up after someone else
- Improving your mind
- De-improving your mind

- Dressing/Undressing
- Washing dishes
- Stalling
- Listening to someone who is not terribly interesting

Timing Miscellaneous Stuff

Most interstate highways have small signs posted every mile, called mile markers. They're small, so you may have to look for them. If you're on a highway that has them, time yourself as you go by each. If you're 60 seconds between markers, you're going 60 miles per hour. If it's 55 seconds, figure 65 mph; 65 seconds, 55 mph.

heck your arm out by heaving a tennis ball into the air. Have someone start the watch the instant the ball leaves your hand and stop it the instant it hits the ground. Use the following chart to see how high it went:

6 seconds ·········► 144 feet

5 seconds ·········► 108 feet

4 seconds ·········► 64 feet

3 seconds ·········► 42 feet

2 seconds ·········► 16 feet

Free Catalogue

he entire library of Klutz books, as well as additional stopwatches and a unique assortment of juggling apparatus, face paints, harmonicas, yo-yos, and who knows what else, are all available in our **Flying Apparatus Catalogue**. The catalogue is free for the asking. Just write us.

Klutz Flying Apparatus Catalogue

2121 Staunton Court
Palo Alto, CA 94306

☎ 415·424·0739